591 SEL 68738

Selsam, Millicent Ellis,
How to be a nature
detective,.

DATE DUE	BORROWER'S NAME	ROOM NUMBER

Teaches the young nature lover how to find and read tracks and clues for dogs, cats, foxes, rabbits, and deer.

Siskiyou County Schools Library
E.S.E.A. TITLE II, PHASE TWO, 1969

68738

[illegible] DETECTIVE

by MILLICENT SELSAM

Pictures by EZRA JACK KEATS

Harper & Row, Publishers New York

Siskiyou County Schools Library
E.S.E.A. TITLE II, PHASE TWO, 1969

HOW TO BE A NATURE DETECTIVE

Text copyright © 1958, 1963 by Millicent Selsam
Pictures copyright © 1963 by Scholastic Magazines, Inc.

This edition published 1966 by Harper & Row, Publishers, Incorporated, in cooperation with Scholastic Magazines, Inc. The text was originally published in different form under the title *Nature Detective.*

Printed in the United States of America. All rights reserved.

Library of Congress Catalog Card Number: 66-15947

and John and Vicky Eisen, Jerry and Moira Fried, Gregory Hunt, Ann Joseph, Adam and Mary Lou Kabat, Johnny Kurtz, Richard and Larry Polatchek, Lisa and Rebecca and Billy Schilit, Jack and Danny Schiller, Ellen and Mark and Judy Shapiro, Jonathan Vall, Liz and Susie Waller, Kenny and Terry Wolfson.

"Where did he go?"

A detective has many ways to find out.

Siskiyou County Schools Library
E.S.E.A. TITLE II, PHASE TWO, 1969

One way is to look for the marks
someone or something has made—
fingerprints,
footprints,
the tracks made by car tires.

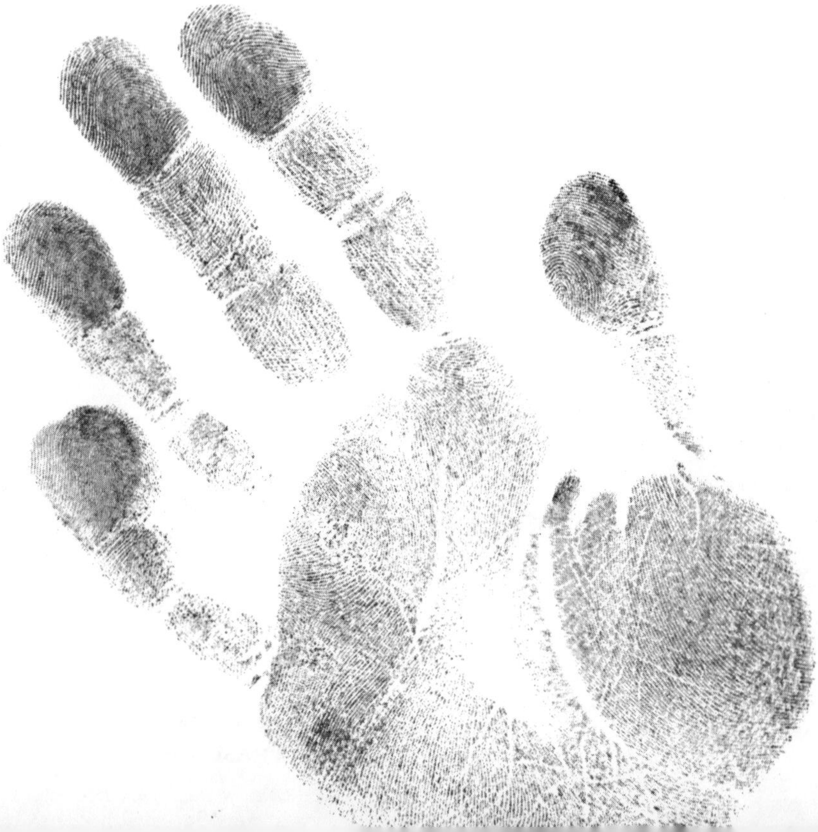

Sometimes a detective finds

What happened?

Who was here?

Where did he go?

Sometimes mothers are good detectives.

You can be a detective too,
a special kind of detective—
a nature detective.

Nature detectives find tracks and clues that answer *these* questions:

What animal walked here?

Where did it go?

What did it do?

What did it eat?

Where does a nature detective look for clues? Almost anywhere—in a backyard, in the woods, in a city park.

You can find tracks in many places — in mud, in snow, in sand, in dust, even on the sidewalk or on the floor.

Wet feet or wet muddy paws can make a track anywhere.

Here is a problem for a nature detective:

Here is a cat.

Here is a dog.

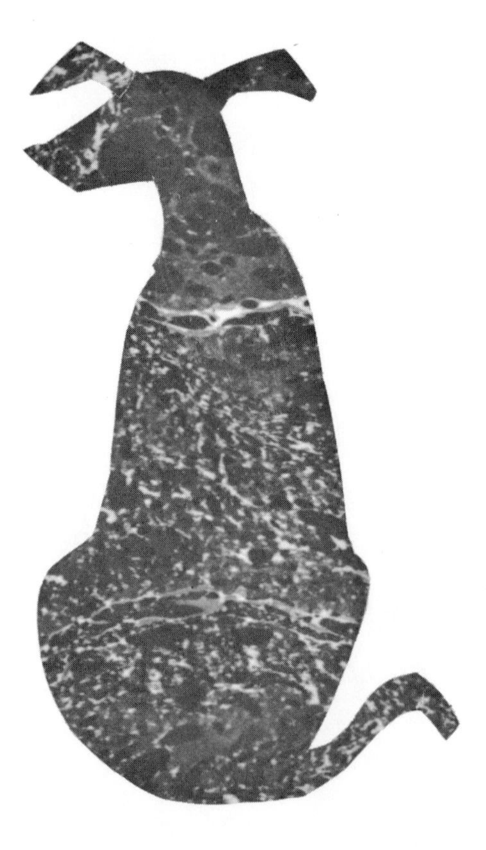

The dog's dish had meat in it.

Who drank the milk? Who ate the meat?
Look at the tracks and see.

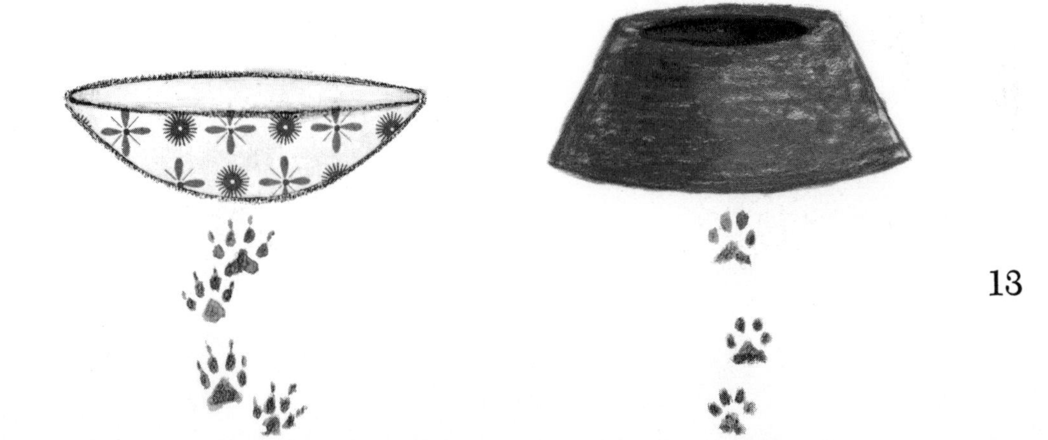

Look at the tracks that go to the *cat's* dish. They were made by an animal that walks on four feet. And you see claw marks in front of the toe marks.

A cat has four feet and sharp claws. But so does a dog.

Who went to the cat's dish?
We still don't know.

Let's look for more clues.

Now look at the other tracks — the tracks that go to the *dog's* dish.

Did you ever watch a cat walk?

A cat walks on four feet. But the

[illegible]

animal with only two legs.

A cat pulls his claws in when he walks.
That is why he does not leave claw marks.

Now do you know

who drank the milk? (THE DOG!)

who ate the dog food? (THE CAT!)

Tigers and panthers make tracks in a single line, just like the cat.

Most of you won't be tracking tigers and panthers. But you may see fox tracks.

The footprints of a fox are in a single line, like a cat's footprints. But they have claw marks, like a dog's.

What kind of footprints will a rabbit make? You can see that a rabbit has little front paws and big hind feet.

The little front paws will make little paw prints, like this:

The big hind feet will make big tracks, like this:

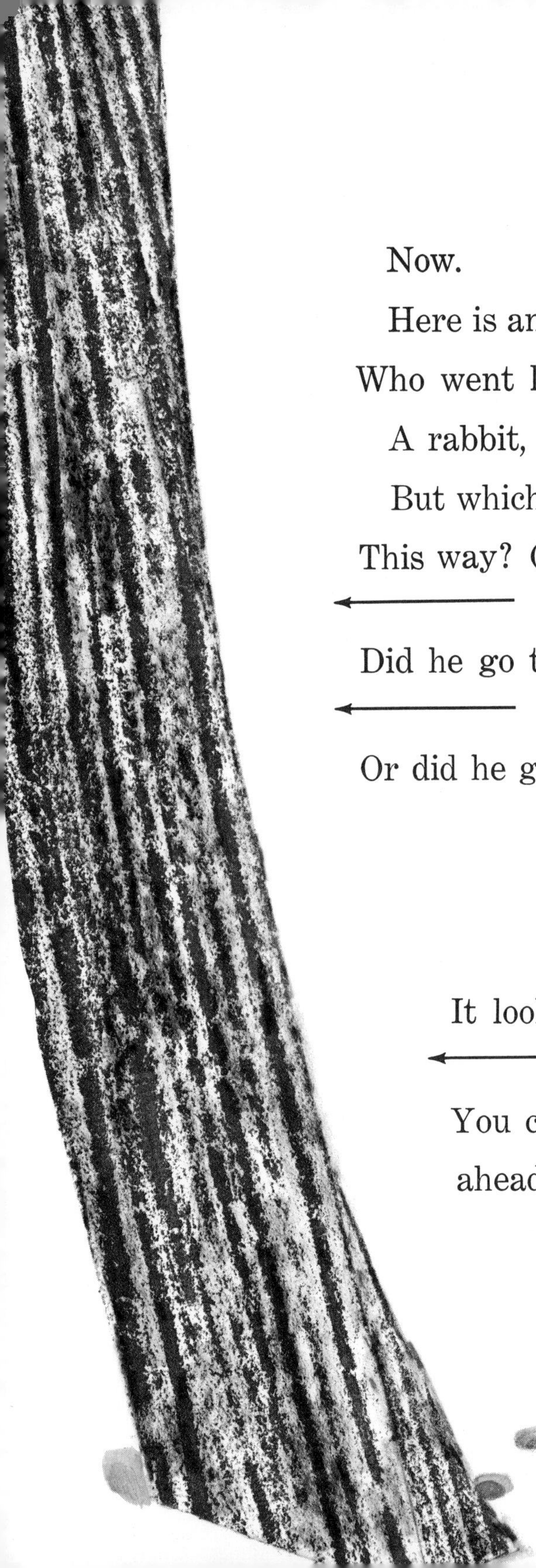

Now.

Here is another problem for a nature detective: Who went lickety-split across the snow?

A rabbit, of course.

But which way did he go?

This way? Or this way?

←——— ———→

Did he go to the tree?

←———

Or did he go away from the tree?

———→

It looks as if he went this way, doesn't it?

←———

You can see the marks of the front paws ahead of the big hind feet.

But do you know how a rabbit jumps? Look at that!

When a rabbit jumps, he puts his big hind feet ahead of his front paws.

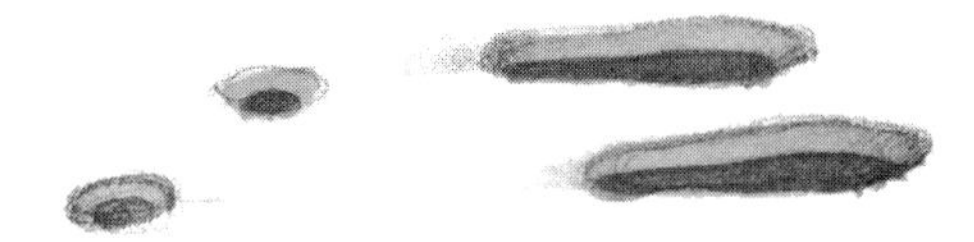

What happened here on a snowy day?

You can see the rabbit tracks in the snow.
You know that they are going this way. →
All at once the rabbit tracks are far apart.
That means the rabbit began to take big jumps.

He was in a hurry.
Why?

Who could have made those tracks?
There is only one answer....

A fox!

Now you know why the rabbit was in a hurry!

Did the fox catch the rabbit? Look again at the picture on page twenty-five. Look carefully.

There are big hoofprints in the mud near the river. And there are little hoofprints, too.

It was a mother deer and her baby fawn. They came to the river for a drink.

Somebody sat down on the muddy bank
of the river.
Who?

And somebody made these tracks
that go right into the water.

A bullfrog came out of the river.
He sat on the muddy bank to rest.

And only a snake leaves tracks like this.
A snake came down to the river. Then he slithered into the water.

The tracks look something like the hands and feet of a baby. But look at those long claws! A raccoon made those tracks. Raccoons like to catch crayfish and eat them.

Siskiyou County Schools Library
E.S.E.A. TITLE II, PHASE TWO, 1969

So now you know what happened.

A raccoon had dinner here last night. He found crayfish in the river. He ate the crayfish. And he left the shells in a little pile.

What's going on here?

This is what's going on!

A nature detective can find many clues on a sandy beach.

When you walk on the beach in the morning, look for the seagull tracks. They can tell you which way the wind was blowing when the gulls were there.

Like airplanes, seagulls take off facing into the wind. First the gulls must run along the sand to get up speed for a take-off. As they run, their toes dig deeper into the sand.

Here all the gull toe tracks are in a line facing east. So you know that the wind came from the east.

Tracks are good clues for a nature detective. But there are other clues, too.

A nature detective learns to look and listen — and smell.

He can find clues in a backyard, in the woods, or in a city park.

Who ate here?

Who lives here?

Who went by?

Do you know who made these tracks?

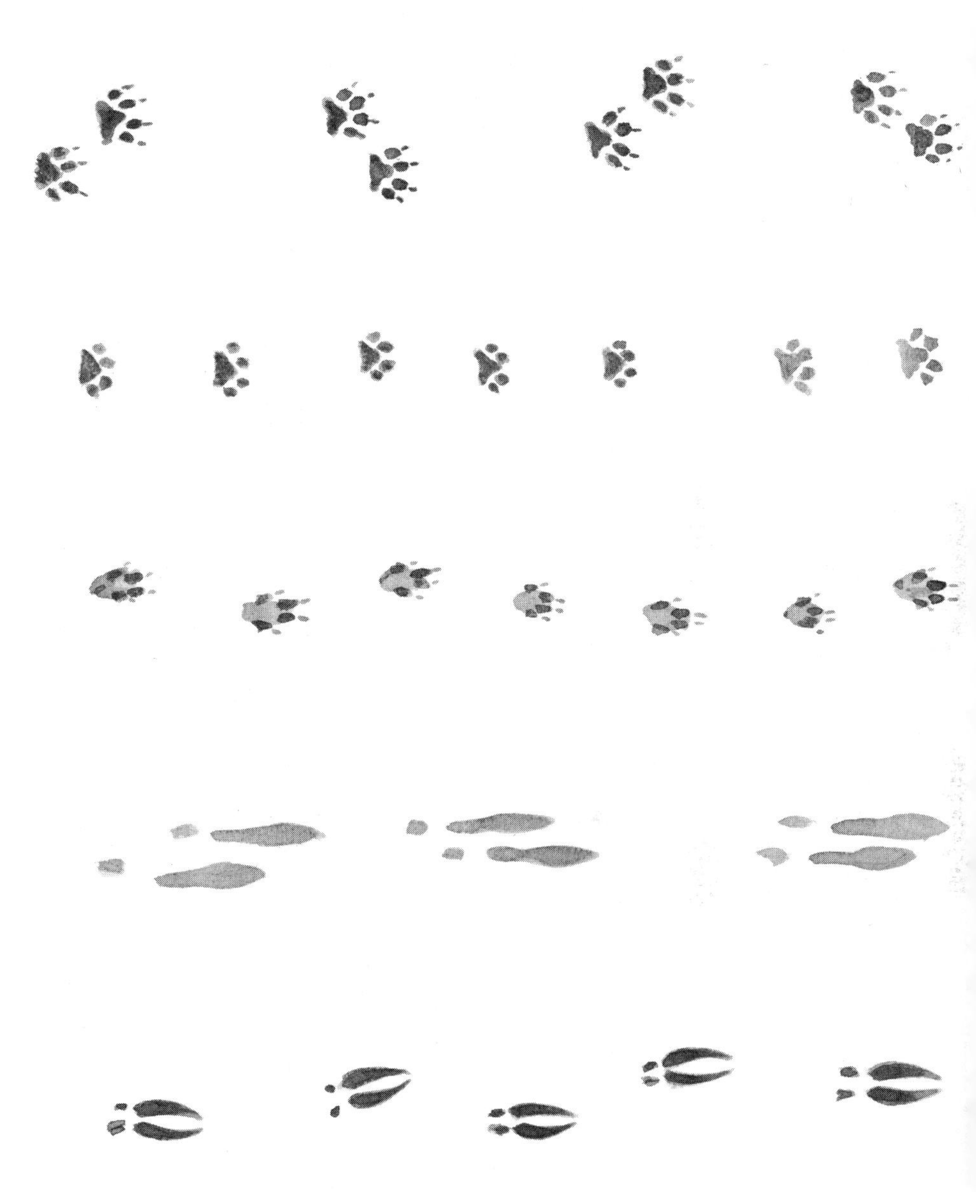

Follow the tracks and see.

Dog
Cat
Fox
Rabbit
Deer

And who made these tracks?

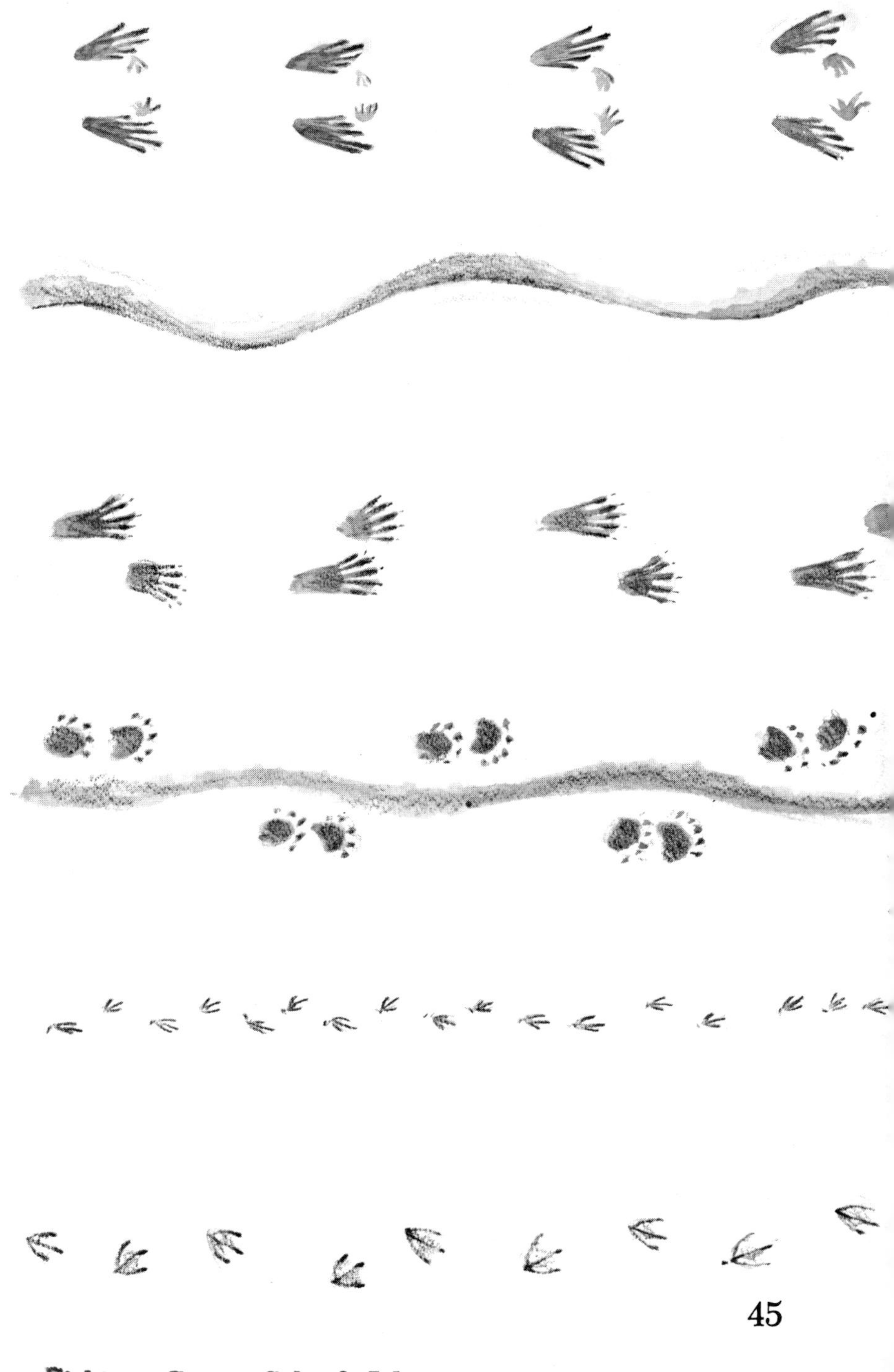

Siskiyou County Schools Library
E.S.E.A. TITLE II, PHASE TWO, 1969

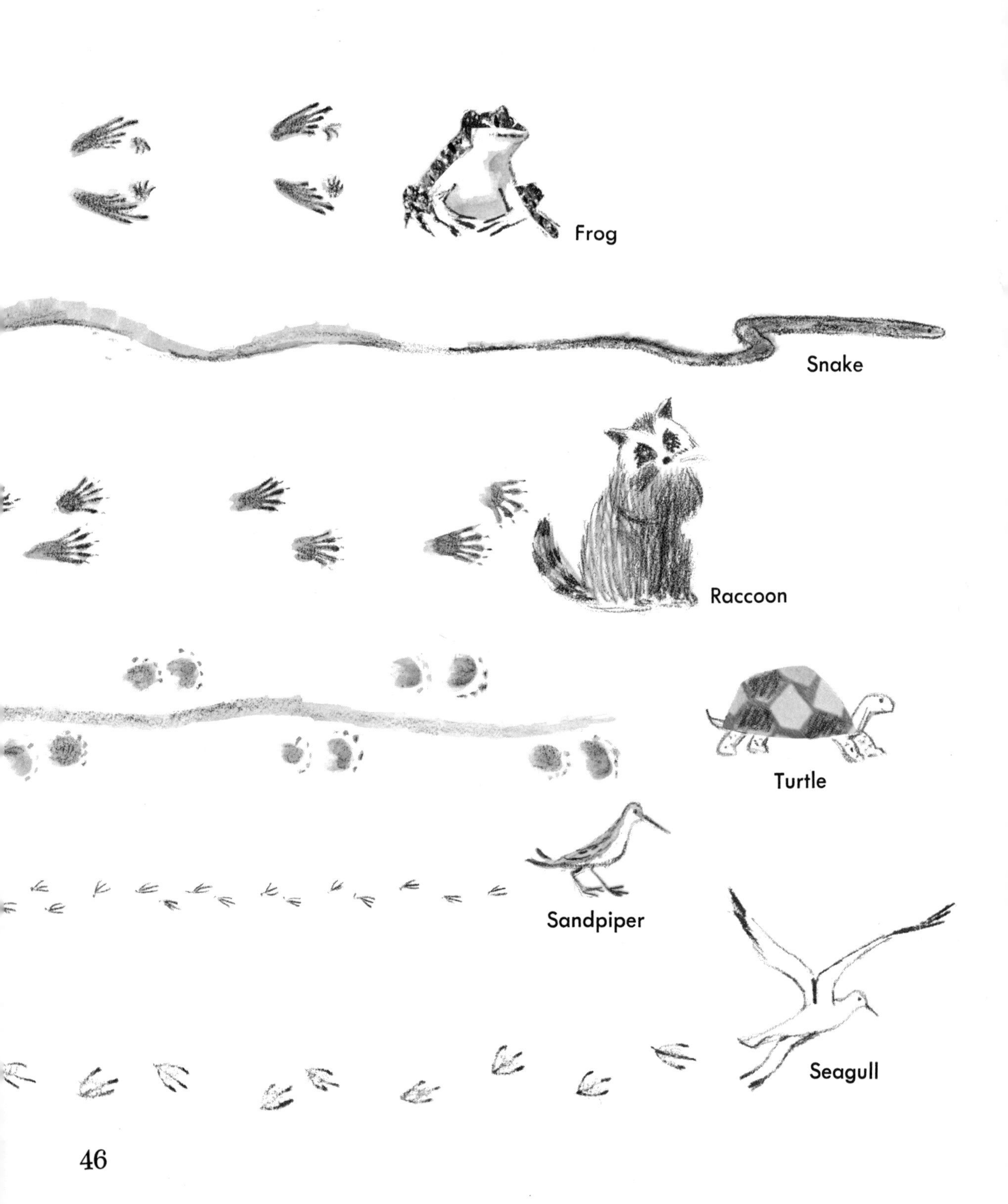
Frog
Snake
Raccoon
Turtle
Sandpiper
Seagull